Your Local Environment

Sally Hewitt

Trimble County Library
P.O. Box 249
Bedford, KY 40006

12-26-08

Crabtree Publishing Company
www.crabtreebooks.com

Crabtree Publishing Company
www.crabtreebooks.com

Author: Sally Hewitt
Editors: Jeremy Smith, Molly Aloian
Proofreaders: Adrianna Morganelli, Crystal Sikkens
Project editor: Robert Walker
Production coordinator: Margaret Amy Salter
Art director: Jonathan Hair
Design: Jason Anscomb
Prepress technician: Katherine Kantor

Activity pages development by Shakespeare Squared
www.shakespearesquared.com

Picture credits: Alamy: pages 6 (top), 7, 8, 10 (top), 13 (bottom), 18, 19 (bottom), 21 (center right), 22, 26-27; Dore Primary School: page 11; istockphoto: page 16 (top); Kids for Tigers: page 23; Project Clean Sweep: page 15; Ripple Africa: page 16 (bottom); Sherman Elementary School: page 9; Shutterstock: pages 5, 6 (bottom), 10 (bottom), 12, 13 (top), 14, 18 (bottom), 19 (top), 21 (center left); Southfields Primary School: page 24; UNICEF: page 17
Every attempt has been made to clear copyright. Should there be any inadvertent omission, please apply to the publisher for rectification.

Library and Archives Canada Cataloguing in Publication

Hewitt, Sally, 1949-
    Your local environment / Sally Hewitt.

(Green team)
Includes index.
ISBN 978-0-7787-4100-8 (bound).--ISBN 978-0-7787-4107-7 (pbk.)

    1. Environmental responsibility--Juvenile literature.
2. Environmental protection--Juvenile literature. I. Title. II. Series:
Hewitt, Sally, 1949- . Green team.

GE195.7.H49 2008   j333.72   C2008-903494-5

Library of Congress Cataloging-in-Publication Data

Hewitt, Sally, 1949-
  Your local environment / Sally Hewitt.
     p. cm. -- (Green team)
  Includes index.
  ISBN-13: 978-0-7787-4100-8 (reinforced lib. bdg. : alk. paper)
  ISBN-10: 0-7787-4100-1 (reinforced lib. bdg. : alk. paper)
  ISBN-13: 978-0-7787-4107-7 (pbk. : alk. paper)
  ISBN-10: 0-7787-4107-9 (pbk. : alk. paper)
 1. Environmental responsibility--Juvenile literature. I. Title.
II. Series.

  GE195.7.H49 2009
  333.72--dc22

                 2008023292

Crabtree Publishing Company
www.crabtreebooks.com   1-800-387-7650

Copyright © **2009 CRABTREE PUBLISHING COMPANY**.
All rights reserved. No part of this publication may be reproduced, stored in a retrieval system or be transmitted in any form or by any means, electronic, mechanical, photocopying, recording, or otherwise, without the prior written permission of Crabtree Publishing Company. In Canada: We acknowledge the financial support of the Government of Canada through the Book Publishing Industry Development Program (BPIDP) for our publishing activities.

Published in Canada
Crabtree Publishing
616 Welland Ave.
St. Catharines, Ontario
L2M 5V6

Published in the United States
Crabtree Publishing
PMB16A
350 Fifth Ave., Suite 3308
New York, NY 10118

Contents

Your local environment

Your local **environment** is your neighborhood. Whether you live in a city, a town, by an ocean, or in the country, you share your local environment with other people, plants, and animals. It is important to look after it.

This family lives in a city. The neighbors on their street all help to make it a nice place to live.

Challenge!

Find out about the people, animals, and plants that share your local environment.

- What can you do to be helpful and friendly to your neighbors?
- How can you help to keep your neighborhood clean and safe?
- What could you do to look after local wild animals and plants?

Mr. Tiddles

Mr. Tiddles, the pet cat, has a bell on his collar. It warns local birds and small animals to run away when he goes hunting.

Students enjoy coming into a clean, bright school.

These children are enjoying the wildlife that lives in the trees and other plants in their schoolyard.

At school

Your school is part of your local environment. Keeping it clean, safe, and attractive is good for everyone who works there. You can help to make sure it's good for the planet, too (see page 9).

Keeping tidy

Litter makes a school look messy and uncared for inside. It can get into drains and harm wildlife outside.

Your school

Your school shares its neighborhood with people, animals, and plants, too. You can help to make sure your school is doing its best to care for the local environment.

Action!

- **Encourage** your school to use **eco-friendly** cleaning products. Powerful chemicals in some cleaning products can harm the environment.
- Have a weekly competition for the cleanest, tidiest, brightest classroom.
- Make sure your school is litter free inside and outside.

The schoolyard

A schoolyard can be a safe place to play or relax in between classes.
It might have space to run and kick a ball, somewhere to sit in the shade,
monkey bars, or even a garden.

There is somewhere for all the students to play in this schoolyard. Is it a good place for plants and animals?

Challenge!

Hold a schoolyard survey. Find out:

- What kinds of different spaces there are in your schoolyard.
- Are there places where plants and animals can grow and live?
- Could your schoolyard be improved?
- What could you do to improve it?

Action!

Send out a questionnaire. Ask:

What do you like about the schoolyard?

What don't you like?

Is it good for the students?

Is it good for plants and animals?

Is it good for the planet?

How would you like to see it improved?

Draw a plan of your "dream" schoolyard.

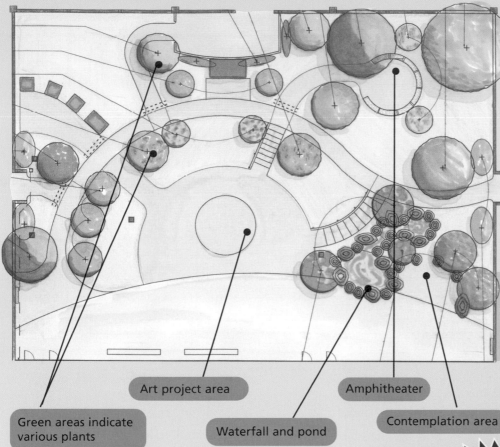

Green areas indicate various plants

Art project area

Waterfall and pond

Amphitheater

Contemplation area

Everyone helped to plan a garden that had activities for students and was good for the environment.

Case study— A green schoolyard

Some schools in San Francisco have been given the chance to change their schoolyards into "green schoolyards." There is space for the children to play, have outdoor lessons, grow plants, and learn about wildlife and their local environment. Everything is built with materials that are friendly to the environment.

Sherman Elementary School, California

At Sherman Elementary School, parents and children designed the schoolyard together (see top). Neighbors helped to build it. Everyone is involved in looking after it.

Asha Chan

"We love our new schoolyard—we get a chance to plant flowers and to watch them grow."

Asha Chan, Sherman Elementary School

Wildlife garden

You can grow plants and encourage animals to visit or make their homes wherever you live. Even if you do not have a garden you can grow plants in pots and window boxes, which will attract insects, birds, and other small animals.

Tidy gardens

There are no places for animals to hide and make their homes in an overly tidy garden like the one shown left. Chemicals used in gardens to kill weeds and insects kill other plants and animals, too. Diagrams called food chains show how we all depend on other organisms in order to survive.

A super tidy garden like this one may look good, but it can be harmful to local wildlife.

A Simple Food Chain

Apple blossom is produced.

Plants are germinated by bees.

Apples are produced. Inside are seeds, which can grow new trees.

Bee picks up pollen from apple blossom.

People, plants, and animals depend on each other to survive. Without insects to carry pollen from flower to flower there would soon be no fruit, vegetables, and seeds to eat.

Challenge!

Can you create a place for wildlife at school or where you live?

- Plant a window box with flowers that attract bees and butterflies.
- Make a pile of rocks where frogs or lizards can hide.
- Make a pile of leaves and twigs for small animals to hide.
- Ban harmful chemicals.

Case study—
Dore Primary School

Dore Primary School in Sheffield, in England, has created a wildlife garden by regenerating an unused area of the school grounds. They cleared it and planted a variety of plants, put up bird houses, and spruced up the bog garden.

 **Action!**

Create a wildlife garden in your schoolyard. If your schoolyard is very small, plant flowers and vegetables in containers and create spaces for animals in unused corners. Learn about plants and animals and their importance for the whole planet.

Alice says: "We had a lot of fun identifying all the plants before we began work on our wildlife garden."

"It was hard work clearing the overgrown garden but it was fun and looked great when we'd finished."

"This was an overgrown area so we're doing something about it. We removed the cow parsley, nettles, and thistles and now you can see the pond again."

"To encourage birds to use the garden, we put up nest boxes around the outside and two on trees in the garden."

"The storms brought down a lot of branches. We are recycling them and using them as seats and path edges."

"Digging out the paths was fantastic but a lot of hard work. We lined the paths and then put down bark chippings from the felled trees that were damaged in the storms."

11

Attracting wildlife

A wildlife-friendly garden does not just involve plants! You can attract wildlife at home or at school in many different ways. Make sure that you do not get unwanted visitors, too!

Most birdbaths only need a small amount of water. Fill it once a day.

Attract birds

A birdbath gives birds somewhere to wash and a drink. It can just be an old dish or plastic container. Put up feeders in a place that only birds can reach. If they are too low to the ground, you may find other animals such as squirrels will help themselves to food put out for the birds!

Endangered animals

In an environment with towns and cities, roads, and modern farms, animals find it difficult to find places to make their homes. Owls, for example, used to nest in old-fashioned farm buildings. Today, owls are becoming **endangered**. Nest boxes provide owls with welcome homes. Place nest boxes where cats and other animals cannot reach them.

An owl box placed high in a tree could encourage owls to nest there.

Goldfish and ducks make a splash of color in ponds. They eat pond insects and their eggs.

Ponds

Ponds attract all kinds of wildlife. Fish swim underwater and frogs, toads, and salamanders live in the water. Around the edges of the pond, insects hover and skim across the water and water birds search for food.

Challenge!

- Find out which animals share your local environment.
- Decide which ones you would like to attract.
- Find the best ways to attract birds, small mammals, frogs, toads, and reptiles.

 Ponds can be dangerous. Only visit a pond with an adult and make sure there is a fence around a school pond.

Action!

Build a pond in your own garden or at school to attract frogs, toads, and pond insects.

- Dig a hole that is deep in the middle and shallow at the edges.
- Line the hole with some old carpet.
- Line the carpet with strong, waterproof pond liner.
- Hold down the edges of the pond liner with big stones.
- Fill the pond with rainwater.
- Plant some water plants.

Sally   Steve   Jemma

A pond can be an outdoor classroom. These children are learning about the frog that has made its home in the school pond!

Litter

Litter is sometimes called "waste in the wrong place." Chewing gum on the pavement, an old sofa dumped by the side of the road, and a plastic bag floating in a lake are all examples of litter. Litter is ugly and dirty and it can be dangerous, too.

Challenge!

Do not be a litterbug!
- Never drop litter.
- When you are out, always put your litter in the garbage.
- Even better, take your litter home with you and get rid of it responsibly.
- Recycle litter whenever you can.
- Try and reduce the litter you make.

Dumping large amounts of litter somewhere other than a landfill is illegal in many countries. It should be taken to a landfill to be buried or recycled.

Dangerous litter

If litter is washed down the drain, it can pollute the water. It can also block the drains and cause floods! Wind and rain carry litter into streams and rivers and then out to sea where it can strangle or choke animals, sea birds, and fish. Broken glass causes cuts and accidents. Food left to rot soon starts to smell and attract flies and rats, which spread germs. Piles of litter can even cause fires in buildings and forests.

Piles of litter burn easily and can start forest fires. Forest fires devastate the animal **community** that lives within them.

Volunteering

Volunteers all over the world give up their spare time to clean up their local environments to make them safer, healthier places for people and animals to live.

Case study— Project Clean Sweep

Clean the Bay is an **organization** working to clear litter from Narragansett Bay and the Rhode Island shoreline on the east coast of the United States. It was started by two sailors worried about the amount of garbage that was growing year by year. Clean Sweep is one of Clean the Bay's biggest projects. During Clean Sweep, 1,450 volunteers of all ages picked up small pieces of litter along the shoreline.

Governor of Rhode Island, Donald L. Carcieri, says, "Project Clean Sweep is a wonderful example of how individual citizens can accomplish great things."

Project Clean Sweep

1. Small pieces of plastic are washed ashore. If it is not picked up, animals could eat it and choke or become poisoned.

4. Volunteers put on strong gloves to collect small pieces of litter in strong paper bags that are biodegradable.

2. Parents and children picked up litter together on a family day out.

3. Bulldozers and lifting gear were used to clear big pieces of litter.

Trees

Trees play an important part in keeping the planet clean and healthy. A gas in the air called carbon dioxide is one of the factors causing climate change. Trees take in carbon dioxide and release oxygen—the gas that we need to breathe.

All over the world, rain forests are being cut down for farming and timber. Where this happens, plants and animals lose their homes and start to die out. Fewer trees means more carbon dioxide in the air.

These beautiful old trees provide shelter for this school in Kenya, Africa.

Wonderful trees

Trees are wonderful! They help keep the air clean. Forests are homes to other plants and animals. Trees give us shade and shelter from the sun and rain, and building materials for our homes. Trees are beautiful. Can you imagine a world without trees?

Sustainable wood

Once cut down, rainforest trees take hundreds of years to grow again, and sometimes a forest is never re-grown. **Sustainable** wood is wood that comes from forests of fast growing trees, such as pine, which are replanted when they are cut down.

Case study— Plant for the Planet

Under the Plant for the Planet: Billion Tree **Campaign**, people, communities, organizations, business and industry, and governments are being encouraged to plant trees and enter their tree planting pledges on a website. The objective is to plant at least one billion trees worldwide every year. Children at the first Africa Region Children's Conference planted 5,000 trees as a contribution to the Billion Tree Campaign in Yaoundé, the capital city of Cameroon.

A boy ready to plant a tree in Cameroon, in Africa.

Challenge!

Find out what is made of wood at home and at school. For example, building materials, furniture, and paper are all made of wood.

When your family or school buy things made from wood, check to see if the wood is from a sustainable forest.

Action!

Plant a tree!

- Choose a tree seedling that is native to where you live.
- Find a suitable place to plant it with plenty of room for the full grown tree.
- Dig a hole deep and wide enough for the roots.
- Plant the seedling and press dirt round it gently and firmly.
- Feed and water it.

Your local park

A park that is clean, free of litter, and full of plants and flowers can be enjoyed by everyone. It is a great place for holding a sports day, a picnic, or a fair where the whole community can get together and have a good time.

Children play together in their local park.

Dog waste

Dog waste is dirty, smelly, and full of germs. If dog waste is left lying around on the grass, germs can be spread and people can become sick. Picking it up helps to keep the park a safer, cleaner place. Paper or cardboard are better for the job than plastic bags are. Paper products are better for the environment.

Challenge!

Take a walk in the park.

- Are there garbages?
- Do people use the garbages?
- Are there weeds?
- Is the playground safe and well looked after?
- Are there benches to sit on?
- Are the trees and flowers well cared for?
- Is it a nice place to play, have a picnic, or go for a walk?

Graffiti spoils the environment for other people.

Graffiti

Graffiti shows disrespect for whatever it is sprayed on. If there is graffiti in the park, you know some visitors are not caring for it properly. Graffiti should be reported to your local council.

A tidy park is a great place for sports such as soccer.

Enjoy your park

Everyone can enjoy a park that is free of dog waste, litter, and graffiti and is full of plants and flowers. Sports teams can play on the grass, children can play in the playground, and families can go for walks safely.

Action!

Get involved with your local park.

- Some parks are in danger of being closed. Is yours? If so, fight to keep it open. Find out how you or your school could help to improve your park.

- Help to make it a place for people to enjoy themselves and for animals to make their homes.

Pollution

The air you breathe, the soil your fruit and vegetables grow in, and the water you drink and wash with are all part of your local environment. All are in danger of being polluted, but there are things you can do to help to keep them clean.

If air, water, and soil are clean, it will help the people, animals, and plants that depend on them to be healthy.

Pollution from tailpipes is harmful to plants and animals.

Polluted air

Chemicals in cleaning sprays, traffic exhaust, smoke from chimneys in houses and factories, and cigarette smoke all pollute the air and are bad for us to breathe. Everyone can help to keep the air cleaner by using natural and eco-friendly cleaners, by walking, cycling, or taking the bus or train, by saving electricity at home and at school, and by not smoking.

Challenge!

Go clean and green at home and school.

You can clean yourself, your home, and your school with eco-friendly products that will not pollute your local environment.

Water

Chemicals from cleaning products are washed down the drain. Fertilizers and weed killers in the soil get into water. All these polluting chemicals have to be cleaned in water treatment plants.

Soil

Chemical fertilizers, and weed, and pest killers get into the soil and into the plants we eat. They harm animals that live in the soil and insects that visit the plants. **Organic** compost enriches the soil. Some plants, such as marigolds, dill, and nasturtium, help to keep pests away naturally.

Toxic waste

When you change to eco-friendly products, do not pour the old products down the drain or just throw them away. They are toxic! Find out how to dispose of them responsibly.

Get to know the signs that let you know which chemicals are dangerous.

Put plants around your home and school. They take in gas called carbon dioxide and other pollutants in the air and release oxygen for you to breathe.

➡ Action!

Natural cleaners

Encourage your parents and your school to use natural cleaners as cheap, alternative cleaners.

- Baking soda cleans and gets rid of smells.
- Corn starch absorbs oil and grease.
- White vinegar and lemon juice clean surfaces.
- Vegetable oil is a polish.

 Warning!

Even natural products are chemicals.

Do not touch anything without adult supervision.

Wear gloves.

Remember! Test natural cleaners on a small area first.

Your community

Your school is part of a community of all the people who live and work in the area. Schools can get involved in local projects and work with people in the community to make it a cleaner, healthier place for everyone.

You can join a local group of volunteers and help to reclaim a local natural area such as a stream, meadow, or forest.

Protecting your environment

The way people live means that the environment around us is in constant threat from the activities of people. Builders and developers are always looking for places to build new houses, while governments look to find space to construct new roads. Find out what the problems are and decide whether you think your local environment is in danger. If you think it is, join a campaign to stop the danger.

Challenge!

Get involved with a community project.

- Find out about an environmental issue that affects your community.
- Work on it with other members of your community.
- Find out if there is an organization that will fund you or give you a **grant**.

Case study—Kids for Tigers

Tigers are in danger. Even though they are protected, poachers shoot them for their beautiful coats, teeth, and bones. Their natural habitat is also under threat. Tigers need space to roam around and hunt for food. Their natural home is in the vast forests of India, but the forests are getting smaller and smaller. Tigers are finding it harder to find enough food to survive.

Saving the forests is an important part of the Kids for Tigers campaign. Kids for Tigers teaches and encourages Indian children to get involved in saving wild tigers and their habitats.

Ananya, Devayani, and Devika Chandra of the Shri Ram School.

"Help! The tigers are dying and all we are doing is watching them die. If we as little children know this, how come adults don't know?"

Kids for Tigers campaign.

1 Walking the Palm Beach nature trail in India, children experienced the amazing scenery, plants, and animals in a tiger's home.

2 Schoolchildren worked together on a long roll of material called a scroll explaining the plight of the Indian tiger.

3 Schoolchildren marched at a Save the Tiger rally in Bangalore.

⟹ Action!

Research which organizations might help you. For example:

- A local wildlife organization
- Woodland or forest organization
- Zoo
- Botanical garden
- Charity
- Local authority
- Other schools
- Local businesses

Making links

Schools make links with each other across the world to support and learn from each other. They find out about each other's local environments, how they affect it, and how it affects them.

Clean water

Lack of water affects plants, animals, and people. Nyogbare Primary School in Ghana is in a dry area. It had no access to clean water. Students at Southfields Primary School in Coventry, in England, who are used to having a lot of clean, running water learned to appreciate the importance of a clean water supply. Both schools worked together to make a difference.

"We are grateful for the concern Southfields have for our brothers and sisters in Nyogbare. The construction of the bore hole is complete and the children, teachers, and communities close to the school are enjoying the water. We are about to start the safe hygiene training in the school."

Gani Tijani, Director of Rural Aid in the Upper East Region of Ghana.

Southfields Primary School in Coventry, in England, linked with Nyogbare Primary School in Ghana. They helped to pay for a water pump for the children to use (above).

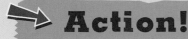

Adopt a habitat

Find out all you can!

- What animals and plants live there?
- What is threatening the habitat you have chosen?
- What can you do to help?
- Join an organization that will help you.

Environments under threat

Many factors threaten local environments such as forests, wetlands, coastlines, and coral reefs. It is important for people to find ways of living and working in harmony with the environment. Here is a list of the ways in which humans can threaten the environment around them.

Coral reefs are under threat from pollution. Tourism can also damage the delicate coral.

Challenge!

Link with a school in another part of the world.

Learn about each other's daily lives and local environments.

Find out how you can work together to improve the lives of the students, animals, and plants in the local environments.

People

There are billions of people on Earth. We are taking up more and more space. We must remember that we share Earth with plants and animals.

Farming

Huge areas of land are cleared to grow crops for food and materials such as wood and cotton.

Industry

We are using up natural resources such as coal, gas, oil, and metal. Pollution from factories, homes, and cars can threaten local environments.

Tourism

People want to travel to beautiful places, but tourists sometimes cause environmental damage. Responsible tourists can help to conserve the places they visit.

Spread the word

You can form a **Green Team** in your school with your friends to help the environment. Share what you have learned with the whole school, parents, and friends. Make sure everyone knows what you are doing.

Challenge!

Make a list of ways you can pass on information.
Make a plan and give yourself a time limit to get everything done.

Make a plan of ways you can make a difference and share it with friends.

Enfield Primary School has set up a Green Team. These members share information with the whole school at an assembly.

Local news

Your local newspaper, radio, or TV station will be interested in local issues and what local schools are doing. Invite them to your special events or send out press releases with photographs.

Green Team members post the latest eco-news on the school website.

Posters

Design posters about your local environment. Put them up at school and get permission to put them up in local stores and libraries. If there is a local event or meeting, put up posters and make sure everyone knows about it.

School website

Do you have a school website? If so, set up a Green Team news page. Keep it up-to-date with information and news about your green projects. Include ideas of how everyone can join in.

Ask your school if you can put up posters to support what you are doing.

 **Action!**

- Hold a school assembly.
- Write and perform a play.
- Have a poster campaign.
- Write newsletters and send them out.
- Post news and information on the school website.
- Send press releases to your local newspaper, radio, or TV station.

Nature at Risk

Help save an endangered plant or animal in your area.

Let's Get Started!

A **species** is a type of plant or animal. All over the world, endangered species are at risk of becoming extinct. If something is extinct, it is gone forever. Are any plants or animals in danger where you live? In this activity, you will use print and online resources to find out. Then you will take action to aid an endangered species.

Activity

1. With a partner, visit a library and find information about endangered plants and animals in your area. Look in books, magazines, or online. If you need help, you can ask a librarian.

2. You might find that several local plant or animal species are in danger. With your partner, choose one to focus on. Make sure to find out why the species is in danger and what can be done to save it.

3. Write a letter to a local politician. Tell him or her about the endangered species and about what must be done to save it. Ask him or her to vote for any bills that would help protect its habitat.

4. Find a volunteer group that works to save the endangered species. You can find such clubs online by typing key words into a search engine. Your teacher or a librarian can also help you find a group.

5. Contact the group and ask how you can help. You and your partner might take part in an event to raise money to help the plant or animal. Maybe you could participate in a short race and collect money from sponsors to help preserve an animal's habitat. You could also take part in an event to teach others about the endangered species. For example, you could hand out information about the species at a booth at a fair.

6. The group might also suggest ways in which you can directly help a species. For instance, with adult supervision, you and your partner might remove **invasive plants** that are taking over a native plant's habitat. Invasive plants are plants that have been introduced to a habitat in which they do not originally grow.

Looking Back

After you complete the activity, answer the following questions. Discuss your responses with your class.

- What did you and your partner learn about endangered species in your area?

- Think about your experiences helping endangered species. Which activity did you feel helped most? Why?

- What problems did you face while trying to help an endangered species?

- What could you do in the future to help endangered species?

Glossary

Campaign
A campaign is action taken to get something done.

Community
A community is all the people who live and work in a neighborhood. Plants and animals are part of the community, too.

Eco-friendly
Eco-friendly means not being harmful to the environment or to the plants and animals that live in it.

Encourage
To encourage means to give help or to persuade someone to do something.

Environment
The environment is everything around you. You might live in a built-up environment such as a city or in a natural environment such as the countryside.

Endangered
Endangered means at risk. Endangered animals are at risk of dying out and becoming extinct.

Grant
A grant is money given to help with a project. A grant is usually given by an organization or the government.

Green Team
A school Green Team is a group of children and staff who work together to protect the planet and the environment.

Organic
Natural, not man-made. Organic farming uses as few chemicals and artificial pesticides as possible, and farmers rear animals without the routine use of drugs.

Organization
An organization is a group of people running a business or a charity.

Sustainable
If something is sustainable, it can be kept going. Using natural resources such as wood or oil in a sustainable way means using it in a way that does not use it all up or destroy part of the natural environment.

Volunteer
A volunteer is somebody who works without being paid.

Websites

www.lcd.org
Link Community Development works to improve education for children and to link schools all over the world.

www.unep.org
The United Nations Environment Program
Its aim is to give leadership and encourage people to work as partners in caring for the environment.

www.wwf.org/
The World Wildlife Fund is an organization that protects animals in their natural habitats all over the world.

www.wwf.org.uk/gowild/index.asp
The World Wildlife Fund for kids.

www.unep.org/billiontreecampaign/
The United Nations Environment Programme (UNEP) has launched a major worldwide tree planting campaign.

www.woodland-trust.org.uk/
Woodland Trust is a conservation charity dedicated to the protection of native woodland heritage in the UK.

www.kidsfortigers.org/
Kids take action to help save tigers in India.

Note to parents and teachers:

Every effort has been made by the Publishers to ensure that these websites are suitable for children, that they are of the highest educational value, and that they contain no inappropriate or offensive material. However, because of the nature of the Internet, it is impossible to guarantee that the contents of these sites will not be altered. We strongly advise that Internet access is supervised by a responsible adult.

Index

Printed in China